The 1st SS ARMORED DIVISION

A Documentation in Words and Pictures

Herbert Walther

1469 Morstein Road, West Chester, Pennsylvania 19380

ACKNOWLEDGEMENTS

To all who helped me with the work on this book, let me express my hearty thanks!

Thanks particularly to Meinrad Nilges and Werner Heid of the Federal Archives in Koblenz, the colleagues of the Imperial War Museum, London, Mr. Jost W. Schneider, Wuppertal, and many of my comrades of the LAH, especially G. Isecke, Ganzmüller and Albert Frey.

Most of all, I thank my dear wife Alice for her great help, tireless work with me, and often-strained patience.

May this book help young people (including my grandsons Jan and Tilo) understand that the men of the Waffen-SS did their duty as soldiers to the bitter end and were condemned, reviled and scorned more than others in return.

PHOTO SOURCES

Federal Archives, Koblenz
Imperial War Museum, London
Jost W. Schneider Archives, Wuppertal
Ganzmüller Archives, Bayreuth
and numerous privately owned pictures

BIBLIOGRAPHY

E. G. Krätschner, "Wearers of the Knight's Cross in the Waffen-SS, K. W. Schütz Publishing (1982)

Jost W. Schneider, "Permission Granted", R. J. Bender Publishing R. Lehmann & Ralf Tiemann, "The Bodyguard", Vol. I/IV2, Munin Publishing, Osnabrück

J. Piekalkiewicz, "The Second World War", ECON 1985 Alan Wykes, "Hitler's Bodyguards", Ballantine Books, London K. Simpson, "The Elite", Vol. 12, Orbis, London

Leo Kessler, "SS Peiper", Leo Cooper, London

Copyright © 1989 by Herbert Walther.
Library of Congress Catalog Number: 88-64001.

Translated from German by Dr. Edward Force.
Printed in the United States of America.
ISBN: 0-88740-165-1
Published by Schiffer Publishing Ltd.
1469 Morstein Road, West Chester, Pennsylvania 19380

This book may be purchased from the publisher.
Please include $2.00 postage.
Try your bookstore first.

CONTENTS

List of Waffen-SS Ranks and their World War 2 German and US Equivalents

Waffen SS	German WW 2 Army	US WW 2 Army
General Officers		
—no equivalent—	Generalfeldmarschall	General of the Army
Oberstgruppenführer	Generaloberst	General
Obergruppenführer	General	Lieutenant General
Gruppenführer	Generalleutnant	Major General
Brigadeführer	Generalmajor	Brigadier General
Staff Officers		
Oberführer	—no equivalent—	—no equivalent—
(wore the shoulder strap of a colonel)		
Standartenführer	Oberst	Colonel
Obersturmbannführer	Oberstleutnant	Lieutenant Colonel
Sturmbannführer	Major	Major
Company Officers		
Hauptsturmführer	Hauptmann	Captain
Obersturmführe	Oberleutnant	1st Lieutenant
Untersturmführer	Leutnant	2nd Lieutenant
Officer Candidates (basically equal to Oberfeldwebel & Feldwebel)		
Oberjunker	Oberfähnrich	—no equivalent—
Junker	Fähnrich	—no equivalent—
Noncommissioned Officers		
Sturmscharführer	Stabsfeldwebel	Sergeant Major
Oberscharführer	Oberfeldwebel	Master Sergeant
Scharführer	Feldwebel	Technical Sergeant
Unterscharführer	Unterfeldwebel	Staff Sergeant
	Unterofficier	Sergeant
Enlisted Men		
—no equivalent—	Stabsgefreiter	Admin Corporal
Rottenführer	Obergetfreiter	Corporal
Sturmmann	Geffreiter	Corporal
SS-Obersoldt *	Obersoldt *	Private 1st Class
SS-Soldat *	Soldat *	Private

*Note: "Soldat" is a general term. Other words used here are Schütze, Grenadier, Füsilier, depending upon the combat arm to which the soldier belonged.

Source of US World War 2 army equivalents: War Department Technical Manual TM-E 30-451 *Handbook on German Military Forces*, 15 March 1945.

Throughout this book, the abbreviation LAH refers to the Leibstandarte Adolf Hitler. The full, official name of this unit at the end of the Second World war was *1st SS-Panzer-Division Leibstandarte Adolf Hitler*. Throughout its existence, the unit had a variety of official names, all of which always contained the phrase *Leibstandarte Adolph Hitler*.

FOREWORD

Since I have been asked again and again how I got the idea of putting together and eventually publishing my book on the Waffen-SS, I would like to utilize the beginning of this volume to offer an explanation.

As a chronicler for the Photo Archives in the Federal Archives at Koblenz, I was able to be of help to many German and foreign writers since 1965 in the choosing and captioning of photographs, most of which had arrived without any details.

I was fortunate enough to find in the Library of the History of the Times in Stuttgart more than 100,000 photographs (24 x 36 mm) taken by war correspondents of the Waffen-SS and mounted in albums. They formed a worthy addition to the approximately one million photographs of the army, navy and air force.

At the request of the publisher Rainer Ahnert, I stated that I was ready to prepare a volume of photographs, "The Waffen-SS". This book appeared in 1972. Textual contributions by Armored Forces General Hasso von Manteuffel, Field Marshal von Manstein, and a closing comment written by Heinz Höhne added to the photo captions.

Now the third volume is finished, and the majority of the pictures in this book are also reproductions of the aforementioned films of the SS Armored Corps. There are also photos which comrades and friends made available, as well as some that were all but unknown and unavailable in Germany, including those from the Imperial War Museum in London.

I have tried to find photos that, if possible, have not been printed before. In writing the photo captions I have tried to mention all recognizable dates, persons and events, often after a long process of asking numerous comrades. For understandable reasons, errors here and there could not be ruled out. Mistaken interpretations and gaps in memories are understandable more than forty years after the events. I thank all the comrades who were of help with information and interpretation, and am naturally also grateful for any details that can be offered.

I have regarded it as my responsibility to make comprehensible the formation and devoted service of the First SS Armored Division "Bodyguard". At the same time, this volume can make clear the accomplishments of the SS photographic correspondents and, not least, document the challenges and sacrifices that fate demanded of this division.

Herbert Walther

Hitler inspects the Bodyguard in the Polish campaign

INTRODUCTION

At the end of World War II the Waffen-SS consisted of 38 divisions. Its manpower numbered about 900,000 men. Thus it was almost twice as strong as the regular German armed forces of the time: army, navy and air force together. As a part of the army, it was subordinate in all its units and in all its service to the command of the German Army.

The Bodyguard—the First Division of the Waffen-SS—was organized and equipped as an armored division. Herbert Walther, the author of this volume and former member of the Bodyguard, has accompanied the division on its way to its fate with his photographic documentation. The many striking photographs give eloquent testimony to the military achievements of the Division and its men.

May this work, along with all previous publications of this kind, serve to clarify to postwar generations the unpolitical, purely soldierly character of the Waffen-SS and its use as a part of the armed forces within the framework of the former German Army.

Albert Frey

THE SYMBOLS

In peacetime: at the Reich Party Day ceremony, 1935.

In wartime: the "Führer's Standard" granted to the LAH, Metz 1940. (BA)

The symbolic figure: SS Lieutenat General Josef "Sepp" Dietrich, Founder and Commander of the Bodyguard.

FORMATION AND TRAINING
1933-1939

Second Company with Fritz
Witt at Jüterlog.

First Public Appearance at the Berlin Sport
Palace, 1933-34. (BA)

In the garrison of the LAH, Berlin-Lichterfelde, May 23, 1935. (BA)

Sepp Dietrich inspects the line. "Gentlemen, present arms!" (BA)

Honor guard detail of the LAH at the funeral of SS Major General Seidel-Dittmarsch, Berlin, 1934. (BA)

Parade formation with rifles hung on their shoulders.

Hitler inspects the Bodyguard at Berlin-Lichterfelde in December of 1935.

The standard and a battalion flag. The LAH now in gray uniforms.

Adolf Hitler and Sepp Dietrich inspect the line. The position in presenting arms has now improved visibly. (BA)

Hitler watches as they march by; at the far right is Sepp Dietrich.

14

Parade in front of
the Chancellery with
white-belted
uniforms. Sepp
Dietrich at the head
of the LAH.

A battalion marches by.

In another parade,
from another perspective:
from left to right: Rudolf
Hess, Sepp Dietrich,
Hitler, Himmler. (BA)

Theodor Wisch, known as "Teddy", as SS Captain and Commander of the First Company of the Bodyguard, ultimately Brigadier General and Division Commander of the First SS Armored Division LAH.

Probably the best-known picture: the First Company with Theodor Wisch in Munich on November 9, 1935.

Theodor Wisch at the head of the LAH honor guard at the 1936 Olympic Games, their first time with white-belted uniforms.

Men of the Bodyguard.

Training of the Motorcycle
Company formed in 1934, still in
black uniforms. (BA)

Combat training with World War I MG 08/15 machine guns, Summer of 1935.

Turning out for sports.

Group picture taken in 1936, with the Commander of the Second Battalion, Jürgen Wagner. (Archives of Jost W. Schneider)

Did these singing young men of the LAH know what lay before them? The black-and-white-rimmed collar insignia and old eagle emblems on the arms of the field-gray uniforms are recognizable.

Two white stripes on the left upper arm for leaders, later also worn on the camouflage jacket.

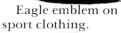
Eagle emblem on sport clothing.

THE POLISH CAMPAIGN
1939

Map of LAH Service

WAFFEN-SS IN POLAND 1939

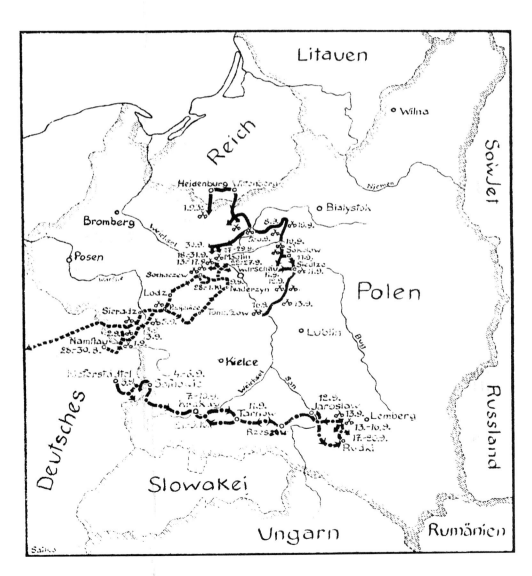

Since there were as yet no war correspondents in service with the Waffen-SS in the Polish campaign, good photographs are rare.

The photos on these two pages, taken by an army war correspondent, show the Bodyguard in battle near Sochaczew, which changed hands several times, on September 15-16, 1939. (BA)

The men of the LAH wear field-gray uniforms and neither camouflage covers on their helmets nor camouflage jackets. (BA)

Hitler in his command car
with Chauffeur Kempka,
General von Reichenau, Hans
Junge and adjutants. (BA)

Adolf Hitler visits the
Bodyguard in Poland.

Sepp Dietrich greets Hitler. From left to
right: Dietrich, Wünsche, Hitler, Schmundt.
(BA)

Hitler inspects the First Company. (BA)

THE WESTERN CAMPAIGN
1940

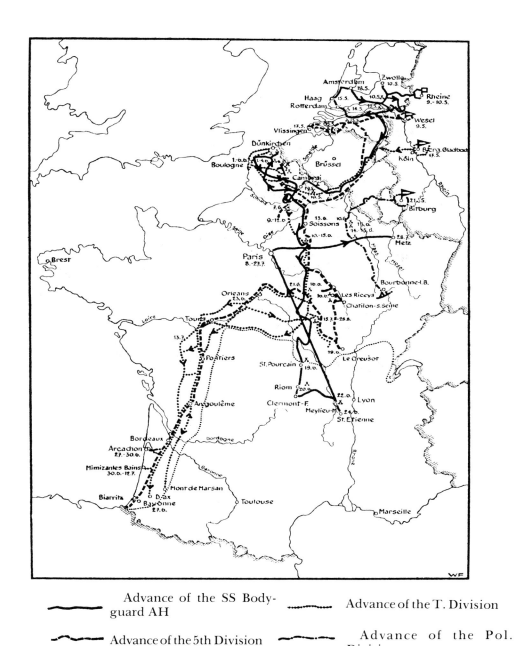

Advance of the SS Body-guard AH

Advance of the T. Division

Advance of the 5th Division

Advance of the Pol. Division

Demarcation Line

The Bodyguard's line of advance in the Western campaign.

Advancing through The Netherlands . . . (BA)

. . . to relieve the paratroopers in Rotterdam.

Through Belgium . . .

. . . and Northern France. The first appearance of Dietrich's tactical symbol.

The "heavy" weapons of the LAH: light infantry guns are set in position. Photographed on May 20, 1940. (BA)

Infantry gunfire supports the infantry's advance. (BA)

3.7 cm antitank gun, later known as the "tank-knocker", in firing position.

The "unknown" Sepp
Dietrich getting dressed in the
morning . . .

. . . and as a great hunter.
(BA)

On-the-spot photograph: a young
dog poses with the regimental
standard of the LAH. (BA)

A 2nd Lieutenant and a Corporal, both decorated with the Iron Cross I. (BA)

The conquest of Clermont-Ferrand, the southernmost point of the advance. (BA)

A Master Sergeant examines captured war materials in the armory works of Schneider-Crussot.

SS 1st Lieutenant Rudolf Lehmann, first of the "Germania" Regiment to be honored with the Iron Cross I on May 29, 1940. (BA)

Later, as Ia, he was the Tactical Leader of the Bodyguard Division. On February 23, 1944 he was decorated with the Knight's Cross, and received the Oak Leaf Cluster on May 6, 1945 as Commander of the 2nd SS Armored Division "The Reich".

Below: Rufolf Lehmann with Otto Baum, ultimately Commander of the 16th SS Armored Grenadier Division, "R. F. SS". (BA)

Jochen Peiper as SS Captain and Company Chief. He told the author that he was quite embarrassed at the time when he saw this picture on the front page of a prominent magazine at all the kiosks in Berlin. (BA)

Himmler inspecting the first armored units (with short-barreled weapons) of the LAH in Metz, summer 1940. The two young Chief Company Leaders, Max Wünsche, left, and Jochen Peiper (with adjutant's insignia), later became the commanders of the armored regiments of the "Bodyguard" Corps. (BA)

When the fighting was over, rest in Metz. Conferring of decorations, here the Iron Cross I for 1st Lieutenant Albert Frey. (BA)

On the march through Metz with the Führer's standard just granted them (at far left, Hein Springer). (BA)

The LAH Honor Guard at the great Victory Parade in Berlin, Section Leader SS 2nd Lieutenant Hans Becker. (BA)

THE BALKAN CAMPAIGN

WAFFEN-SS IN THE BALKAN CAMPAIGN, 1941

━━━━ Advance of the SS Bodyguard A. H.　　━━━ Advance of the SS Division R.

〜〜〜 National Boundaries

The line of advance of the LAH in the
Balkan Campaign.

The LAH, transferred to Rumania as an
instructional troop, in a Heroes' Memorial
Day parade in Campulung on March 16, 1941.

On the march through Bulgaria
to the Yugoslav border at Küstendil
on April 7, 1941. (BA)

The Bodyguard is warmly received and presented with fruit.

Still on good roads for the time being, the southward advance continues quickly. (BA)

But soon the roads grow worse. This requires expert driving and hard physical work.

Orders are given to the First Battalion by Commander Fritz Witt of the "Deutschland" Regiment (decorated with the Knight's Cross on September 4, 1940), returned to the LAH. (BA)

From left to right: Krause, Schulz, Witt, Springer.

Light infantry guns in position. (BA)

A 3.7 cm anti-aircraft gun on its carrier. (BA)

Grenadiers march forward into the field.

The first captured British soldiers. (BA)

Some wear the typical hats of the Australians. (BA)

Mounted grenadiers: onward with . . .

Camouflaged tanks and . . .

. . .armored artillery corpsmen in gray uniforms. (BA)

The
strengthened
reconnaisance
unit of the LAH
under Major Kurt
Meyer
("Panzermeyer")
crosses over to
Patras in a daring
move on April 26,
1941. The
Regimental
Surgeon, Dr.
Besuden, observes
the embarkation
in the harbor of
Nafpaktos. (BA)

A Master
Sergeant
photographs the
event with his
Leica. (BA)

Heavy infantry
guns are loaded,
requiring a lot of
muscle power.
(BA)

Gerd Pleiss, decorated with the Knight's Cross for the storming of the Klidi Pass on April 20, 1941, is interviewed by a war correspondent.

Graves at the Klidi Pass.

Gerd Pleiss with honored men from his First Company. (BA)

Commanders: from left to right Hanreich, F. Witt, Ewert, T. Hansen, ?, Pleiss. (BA)

Himmler visits the Bodyguard in its rest quarters on May 9, 1941 and is greeted with fanfares. (BA)

The "good understanding" between Dietrich and Himmler is clear in this picture. (BA)

Sepp Dietrich in one of his favorite activities. (BA)

In the center of the picture, from left to right: Staudinger, Dietrich, R. Sandig.

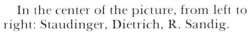

The Bodyguard at rest near Larissa.

While the weapons and a leader rest . . .

. . . the men are commanded: "Potato peelers forward!" One of the men wears a captured Australian hat.

Fritz Witt, in free-time clothes, prepares a smoke. (BA)

"A light for the Commander!" (BA)

"Always a bit of rest and a good cigar!" (BA)

These days of rest and relaxation after days of hard fighting were fully utilized. The young soldiers and their leaders knew that soon they would face even rougher action at greater distances with unimaginable physical demands. After transport into the Brünn area the LAH rolls on to a new position farther to the east and arrives for its first service in Russia on July 2, 1941. (BA)

FIRST RUSSIAN SERVICE
1941-1942

On June 22, 1941 the Russian campaign begins. The "Bodyguard" is leading the fast advance from the start. The 1st Armored Squad supports and pushes them further to the east, then to the south. They go via Uman, Cherson, Mariupol, and Taganrog to Rostov on the Don. In the 1941-1942 winter they are in defensive position on the Mius, and are transferred to France in July of 1942. (BA)

Alle Sinne sind angespannt
Jeden Augenblick kann der vorgehende Stoßtrupp auf den hinter Bäumen und Farren lauernden Feind stoßen
H-PK-Zeichnung · Kriegsberichter Ernst Krause

ILLUSTRIERTE ZEITUNG
Berlin, den 29. September 1942
Nr. 39 XVIII. Jahrgang Preis 20 Pf.
Bulgarien 8 Lewa, Frankreich 4 Francs, Italien 2 Lire, Niederlande 20 Cent, Schweiz 40 Cent., Ungarn 36 Filler

The men with the machine guns, just like the crews of the fighting vehicles (here a mounted 3.7 cm anti-aircraft gun), formed a battle unit in which every man could rely on his comrades. (Lower photo: BA)

What the Armored Corps artist portrays in such a heroic and lively style looks different in grim reality. (BA)

A wounded motorcycle driver is bandaged by his comrades.

Often enough the cycle got "stuck in the mud".

July 9, 1941: the 11th Company of the LAH attacks on the Stalin Line in the woods north of Miropol.

The Company Chief, Albert Frey, with SS Master Sergeant Söhnke, who fell shortly afterward.

Treatment of a wounded man on the battlefield.

SS Staff Sergeant Troschier, who fell as an SS Junior Company Leader and last Leader of the First Company, while under attack before Kharkov.

All photos on this page are by SS Photo Correspondent Augustin.

Muddy roads
and accidents
cannot slow the
advance. They are
overcome by
united efforts.
(BA)

Again and again the infantry tries, often with insufficient means, to strike Russian tanks. The badly wounded SS Junior Platoon Leader Bergemann is brought under cover after he tried to blow up a T 34 tank with a mine. The tank was shot down at point-blank range by the heavy guns of SS 1st Lieutenant G. Isecke shortly afterward. (BA)

In the attack on
Taganrog the Third
Battalion had
partially crossed a
railroad line when
two Russian tank
columns approached
and forced the
battalion to take
cover, firing on both
sides. A 3.7 cm
antitank gun
brought the columns
to a stop, but they
could be defeated
only after a hard
fight. (BA)

The SS Staff Sergeant Oberkofler fell in
this action when he tried to bring up
heavy weapons on his own initiative.

The Russian tanks are inspected by
Lieutenant General Sepp Dietrich.

Battle on the wide plains . . .

An 8.8 cm anti-aircraft gun in position, the best weapon to use against the Russian T 34 tanks that appeared in ever-greater numbers. (BA)

Again and again, prisoners are brought in. (BA)

A 5 cm antitank gun is towed into position. (BA)

. . . and in narrow city streets.

A 3.7 cm anti-aircraft gun in a firefight. (BA)

Tanks (7.5 cm short) supported the infantry. (BA)

The Reconnaissance Unit of the LAH in battle near Mariupol. (IWM)

In their winter position on the Ssambek. From left to right: Keilhaus, Dietrich, "Panzermeyer". Their caps are definitely not from the supply depot.

By now Sepp Dietrich had been decorated with the Oak Leaf Cluster to the Knight's Cross (December 31, 1941). (BA)

Awarding decorations at the cessation of fighting in the fall of 1941. (BA)

Sepp Dietrich congratulates Albert Frey on his "German Cross in Gold", November 17, 1941. (BA)

54

TRANSFER TO FRANCE
1942

The rail transport of the LAH from Russia to France, July 12-18, 1942. More than 200 trains were needed to transport the Division. (BA)

Men of the Third Company, Armored Fusilier Unit, LAH. In the center of the picture is Rudi Roy, later decorated with the Knight's Cross.

War correspondents of the LAH.

Unloading the 4th Tank Unit of the LAH near Melun. (BA)

In the foreground is the Commander, Major Schönberger, who was always called "Schonberger" in the LAH. His reputation was founded on his close friendship to Sepp Dietrich and Heinrich Himmler. He was awarded the Knight's Cross posthumously.

The great parade of the First SS Armored Division "Bodyguard", on the Champs Elysées, Paris, July 29, 1942.

SS Lieutenant General Paul Hausser, Field Marshal von Rundstedt, and SS Senior Squad Leader Sepp Dietrich watch the parade.

SS 1st Lieutenant R. von Ribbentrop, Section leader in the 6th SS Armored Regiment 1 (right).

Sepp Dietrich awards well-earned decorations to the Second Regiment in Russia. In the center of the picture is the Commander, SS Lieutenant Colonel Theodor Wisch, already (September 15, 1941) decorated with the Knight's Cross.

The First Battalion, First Regiment, with Commander Major Albert Frey and Adjutant Hein Springer, passing in review.

Albert Frey with his wife Lotte, on furlough at home in Heidelberg.

The III/1st Regiment with Max Hansen (still Captain) and Adjutant Meyer.

The infantry emblem.

SS Captain Hein Springer, decorated with the Knight's Cross on January 12, 1942, on furlough at home.

His daughter is happy to see the pictures of Papa and the "glittering thing" around his neck.

Armament Minister Albert Speer examines the English tanks captured near Dieppe.

The official report says: "On August 29, 1942, Minister Speer rode with Sepp Dietrich to Dieppe, where he examined the remains of the English attempt to land. He took the opportunity to drive the Churchill tank, to acquaint himself with the characteristics of this English weapon."

Minister Speer told the author: "We were very relieved to learn that the English had remained far behind our developments in tank construction. Thus we had time to test our new tank (Panther) in peace and put it into service just right!" This took place almost a year later in the fighting around Kursk.

From left to right, General Kuntzen, Colonel Thomale, Sepp Dietrich, Minister Speer with his adjutant, General Fichtner of the Military Weapons Office, at right with the hat General Manager Pleiger, chief of the "Hermann Göring Works".

The new assignment
involved much
organizational work for
the Commander, his Ia
R. Lehmann, and
Adjutant Battalion
Leader Schiller.

Sepp Dietrich,
with his knowledge
and experience as an
armored specialist in
both World Wars,
was often asked for
his factual advice, for
example, by Minister
Speer, Field Marshal
von Rundstedt and
Senior General
Haase. (BA)

Senior General
Wilhelm Haase is
well remembered by
all the members of
the LAH for his
humor-filled daily
orders, for example:
"In my army there
was a Captain
Wunderlich who
really was
'wunderlich'
(amazing)", etc.
(BA)

SECOND RUSSIAN SERVICE
SPRING 1943

After a twelve-day railroad trip, the advance command of the LAH arrived at the station in Chucuyev on January 22, 1943. The Ia, Major R. Lehmann, prevented the blowing up of this important unloading depot, as had been planned. By the end of the month the greatest part of the Division had arrived and been thrown directly into the battle. Temperatures of more than 20 degrees below zero, snowstorms and the difficulties they caused reconnaissance placed the highest demands on the young grenadiers, for once again the infantry had to bear the heaviest burdens of the fighting. (BA)

Completely exhausted, the men sink down for a short rest in the snow. (BA)

The fully motorized Division sometimes became horse-drawn, so great were the losses and breakdowns of motor vehicles. (BA)

The heavy-weapons support of the hard-pressed infantry was especially important in order to bring the attacking Russian troops to a stop as quickly as possible.

The 2 cm anti-aircraft gun in position on the ground was a weapon feared by the enemy because of its rapid firing and long range. (BA)

Longer-range
weapons of
larger calibers
likewise reduced
the pressure and
worked
successfully
against the
attacking masses
of Russian
soldiers. Light
howitzer 18 and
infantry guns in
action. (BA)

The heavy Armored Fusilier Unit of the LAH saw its first action. Their stringent weapons and combat training bore fruit. Again and again the command came: "Armored Fusiliers forward!"

The Company Commanders Wöst and Tirschler on the way to a unit discussion, very handy and speedy self-propelled guns roll forward. (BA)

The T 34 tank, appearing in ever-greater numbers, was the chief opponent of the Armored Fusiliers. All in all, it was by far the best of all tanks used in World War II. Its greatest disadvantage, to be sure, was that its commander had to shoot simultaneously. (BA)

Corpsman Reichel of the 1st SS Armored Fusilier Unit of the LAH could record ten scores (as white lines painted) on his gun barrel. A great achievement, particularly when one considers that he was far inferior to the Russian tanks not only in weaponry but also in terms of the armor of his "Marten", which was more than 2.6 meters high. He was decorated with the Iron Cross I and promoted to SS Staff Sergeant. (BA)

Reichel is interviewed by war correspondents.

The Artillery Unit of the LAH, now armed with the long 7.5 cm KWK guns, was generally divided among the companies and sections of the infantry commanders. Experienced commanders knew how to utilize their weapons excellently. It is only natural that many of them later were very successful as armored commanders. The best example is Michel Wittmann, the most successful armored commander of World War II.

The grenadiers liked to stay in the cover of the armored vehicles, but by doing so they drew the enemy's concentrated fire upon themselves. (BA)

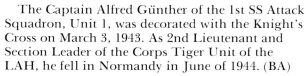

The Captain Alfred Günther of the 1st SS Attack Squadron, Unit 1, was decorated with the Knight's Cross on March 3, 1943. As 2nd Lieutenant and Section Leader of the Corps Tiger Unit of the LAH, he fell in Normandy in June of 1944. (BA)

One of the last pictures of the well-known armored corps photographer Augustin shows the tank of 1st Lieutenant Hans Siegel, who was severely wounded in Kharkov. Decorated with the Knight's Cross at the front, he led the 2nd Unit of the SS Armored Regiment 12 HJ to the bitter end.

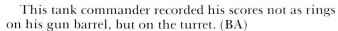

This tank commander recorded his scores not as rings on his gun barrel, but on the turret. (BA)

The Panzer men received winter overalls that were gray on one side and white on the other, but they did not stay that way for long. (BA)

The Armored Regiment was equipped in part with Panzer III tanks. These were superior to the Panzer IV in speed and handling, but too weakly armed with their 5 cm KWK guns.

The Panzer IV tank was the equal of the Russian T 34, above all in firepower. Was the ox roused by the tank's shots?

The Commander of the 1st Unit, SS Armored Regiment 1 LAH, Major Wünsche, directs the tanks and amphibians of the reconnaissance unit. The two units were usually in action together. Max Wünsche received the Knight's Cross on February 28, 1943, and found a practical way to wear it. (BA)

The SS Staff Sergeant Hans Reimling was also decorated with the Knight's Cross on February 28, 1943, particularly because he always drove at the head of the tank unit. A few days later, on March 4, 1943, he fell before Valki. (BA)

Grenadiers attack with armored support. (BA)

Radio transmission of news was often the only means of keeping the units in touch with each other, and was indispensible for directing the troops in the snow-covered vastness.

Whether a small radio troop of the Reconnaissance Unit, once again far forward in a counterattack, . . .

. . . or a big radio vehicle with a bowed antenna plus a long, extending telescopic antenna, all did their best to maintain radio connections among the widely scattered battle groups. (BA)

The fast transport of badly wounded men to field hospitals was necessary for survival in the bitter cold. The true spirit and comradeship of the troops was shown in their care of the wounded. (BA)

The harshness of winter war can be read in the faces of these grenadiers, who nevertheless have not forgotten how to smile.

The tried and true Commander of the 1st SS Armored Grenadier Regiment 1, LAH, Albert Frey, received the Knight's Cross on March 3, 1943.

Hermann Dahlke received the Knight's Cross at the same time, as SS Staff Sergeant and Company Troop Leader of the 3/1st Regiment. He fell, as SS 2nd Lieutenant and Corps Leader, on July 5, 1943.

These two pictures
show the improvizations
and the imaginative
practicality of the troops.

"Panzermeyer",
meanwhile accorded the
Oak Leaf Cluster (on
February 23, 1943),
observes an attack, away
from the motion of his
A.A.

After the grenadiers overwhelmed the strong defensive positions in hard fighting, the tanks of the LAH rolled into the large city of Kharkov from the north. (BA)

A film reporter records for the weekly newsreels the advance of the LAH tanks during street fighting. (BA)

Engineers remove tank obstacles and bridge bomb craters so the tanks can get through. (BA)

Below: A very serious Major Max Hansen, nd Commander of the 3rd SS Armored Grenadier Regiment 1, during preparation for the breakthrough to "Red Square", for which he received the Knight's Cross on March 28, 1943. (BA)

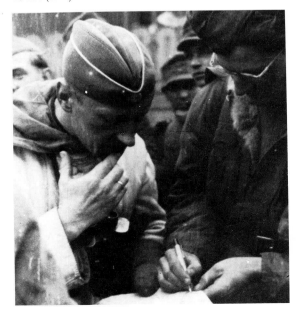

Grenadiers and an armored fusilier tank in the battle for "Red Square" in the center of Kharkov. (BA)

The Commander of the First Regiment, Colonel Fritz Witt (who received the Oak Leaf Cluster to his Knight's Cross on March 1, 1943), and the Commander of the III/2nd Regiment (SPW), Jochen Peiper (in the background the Commander of the Attack Squadron Unit, Major Hein von Westernhagen), meet at "Red Square", which was soon renamed "Bodyguard Square". (BA)

The Peiper battle group turns off to the east to make contact with the A.A., which was involved in heavy fighting on the east side of the city. On account of the blown-up bridge and the concentrated deployment of Siberian sharpshooters, the battle for the "Peiper Bridge" was decisive in the final capture of the city. (BA)

The Armored Fusilier Detachment "Bad Boy" of 2nd Lieutenant Herbert Walther on the "Peiper Bridge". When "Sepp" saw the sign, he said: "Leave it up, it's right!" (BA)

This page shows the staff of one of the battle-tested junior leaders in the street fighting. They often led what remained of the companies and smaller battle groups when all the leaders had been lost. (BA)

At right, the Commander of the 7th Company, Armored Regiment 1, SS 1st Lieutenant Rudolf von Ribbentrop, points the way to a position. (BA)

Panzer IV and Armored Fusiliers shoot the way open for the infantry to connect the battle groups of Meyer and Peiper. Thus Kharkov was again in German hands, and the exhausted grenadiers finally had a well-earned rest. (BA)

On March 18, 1943 the Peiper battle group set out about 7:00 A.M. on the road from Kharkov to Belgorod. After breaking through the Russian defensive positions with dive-bomber support, Peiper decided on a bold hussar charge over more than 40 kilometers and reported at 11:45: Belgorod is in our hands." (BA)

The closing announcement of the battle group said: "Enemy loss of tanks: ten T 34, one T 40, one T 60, two General Lee. Our own losses: one dead, six wounded." (BA)

The grenadiers of the SPW Battalion pause for a smoke. The men are happy to have survived the fighting at Kharkov. (BA)

Auch Du zur
LEIBSTANDARTE-⚡⚡
ADOLF HITLER
EINTRITT MIT VOLLENDETEM 17. LEBENSJAHR

Deutscher Junge!

Dich ruft die Waffen-⚡⚡! Der richtige Platz für Dich wird schon gefunden werden, verfügt doch die ⚡⚡ über alle für den modernen Landkrieg nötigen Waffenarten. Wo wir den Feind treffen, nehmen wir ihn an und werfen ihn. In Polen, im Westfeldzug, im Balkanfeldzug und im Kampf gegen den Bolschewismus haben wir das bewiesen. Bist Du ein Kerl und Draufgänger und dem Führer verschworen, dann gehörst Du zu uns.

⚡⚡-Obergruppenführer und
General der Waffen-⚡⚡

Young men from all over Germany answer the call and march past the "File Leader of Stone" with cardboard suitcases and cartons, into the barracks of the Bodyguard in Berlin-Lichterfelde. (BA)

Here their basic training takes place. (BA)

Combat training in the country. (BA)

Spiess sees everything! (BA)

Practice with live hand grenades, whereby there were, alas, often injured men, and even deaths. (BA)

A guard unit in the courtyard of the LAH Barracks, with the Führer-Casino in the background. (BA)

During the war the LAH also supplied the guards at the Chancellery. (BA)

The guard marches out. (BA)

The high point and conclusion of training: **Taking the oath.**

Marching past the Commander of the First Battalion with resounding music.

OPERATION "CITADEL"
JUNE 4-13, 1943

Tiger tanks and grenadiers approach the great tank battle. (BA)

An infantry leader beside a Tiger directs a four-wheel scout car. (BA)

The opposite page shows that the young grenadiers and junior leaders have not forgotten how to laugh despite the grimness of the battle. (BA)

A machine gunner 1 is wounded beside a Panzer III tank of the 7th Company, Armored Regiment 1. Right: Tanks, as ever, are good support for the infantry. (BA)

Tank ditches of the Russian defense lines provide severe obstacles for the tanks. The tank at left has lost part of its armor plate. (BA)

The tank obstacles and natural gullies give the grenadiers cover and protection for a brief pause to catch their breath. (BA)

A machine gunner 1 with his MG 42 waits at the edge of the trench for the command to attack. (BA)

The Russians, informed by their secret service of the beginning of action and the German plans, await the German troops in a heavily staffed defensive system. With 1,300,000 soldiers, 20,000 guns and mortars, and 3,600 tanks, the Russians are clearly superior in manpower and material. (BA)

"Up and at 'em! Let's attack!" (BA)

For the grenadiers this means coming out of cover into the open fields behind the attacking tanks to hold and secure the captured terrain. (BA)

Badly wounded men are brought back, given first aid, and sent to the main hospital. (BA)

While slightly wounded men remain with the troops, doctors and medics care for the badly wounded in the shelter of a tank ditch. (BA)

The pictures on the left side reflect the tension and the hardness of the tough struggle in the faces and bearing of the soldiers. (BA)

The photo correspondents of the armored corps accompany the advancing troops and catch the action in photographs, in this greatest and probably bloodiest tank battle of World War II, in which several thousand tanks operated in a very limited area. (BA)

Past a disabled T 34 goes the infantry on the attack. (BA)

This infantryman has paused to light his pipe—surely a battle-tested file leader. (BA)

On July 13, 1943, Hitler ordered the cessation of Operation Citadel. Thus the last attempt to achieve freedom of action on the eastern front again was stopped. (BA)

TRANSFER TO ITALY JULY-AUGUST 1943

After brief "emergency intervention" in the southern part of the eastern front, the transfer to Italy took place in July and August of 1943. The tanks remained in Russia. The armored portions, according to an Italian decision, could not be brought over the Brenner Pass in a motorized march, and so had to be loaded onto trains, using many tricks.

As can be seen, the troops solved every transportation problem. At left, an amphibian on top of a halftrack; at right, a captured American Jeep. (BA)

The heavy Armored Fusilier Unit 1 of the LAH made the most of this forced delay in Innsbruck by suitably honoring their first men to wear the Knight's Cross, including an Austrian.

The SS Master Sergeant Kurt Sametreiter received the Knight's Cross on July 31, 1943 for holding off an attack by 40 Russian tanks; his section destroyed 24 tanks and then beat back the Russians with an infantry attack. The two pictures were taken about three months apart.

Werner Wolff, the battle-tested adjutant to Jochen Peiper (Third Armored SS Armored Grenadier Regiment 2 "LAH"), took over a leaderless company and stopped a massive enemy tank attack in which thirty Russian tanks were destroyed in close combat.

For this he was decorated with the Knight's Cross on August 7, 1943. Wolff fell in March 1945 near Junota, Hungary, as Commander of the 7th Company, SS Armored Regiment 1"LAH".

A correspondent of the SS Armored Corps, dressed—interestingly enough—in a black Armored Corps uniform, interviews Werner Wolff after the awarding of the Knight's Cross. The pictures indicate how dramatically he described the action on the radio.

The Commander of the SS Armored Grenadier Regiment 2 "LAH", Lieutenant Colonel Hugo Kraas, confers combat ribbons, at right on the Commander of the I/2nd Regiment, Captain Hans Becker, who fell on the invasion front on August 20, 1944. (BA)

Vehicles of the SS Armored Grenadier Regiment 1 at the northern edge of Milan, where they waited for several days. Meanwhile the Commander, Albert Frey, succeeded through clever, delaying negotiations in persuading the commanding general of an Italian armored corps to surrender. Thus a great bloodbath was avoided, particularly when one considers that Frey had been commanded to break any resistance, if necessary by using bombers, if the overwhelmingly communistic population of Milan was armed and ready to fight.

The Third Armored SS Armored Grenadier Regiment 2 marches unarmed and singing through Reggio-Emilia. At its head, from left to right: Guhl, Peiper, Wolff. For security reasons, armored vehicles were kept ready in the side streets.

Italian soldiers and officers lay down their arms.

Most of them were glad that the war was over for them. Noteworthy opposition occurred, among other places, in Parma, with its large barracks and a renowned officer school. (BA)

The decisive event was the freeing of Mussolini, who had been seized on the Gran-Sasso.

Otto Skorzeny, at that time a member of the LAH, had learned of his capture and led the daring mission.

From left to right: Skorzeny, Lt. Gerlach, who flew the Fieseler "Stork", Mussolini, Karl Radl, Adjutant, and in civilian clothes the Police General Gueli, who had also been captured.

THIRD RUSSIAN SERVICE 1943-1944

Since things were getting hot in Russia again—the Russians were attacking on a broad front—the LAH was rushed to the eastern front to put out the fire. (BA)

The condition of weapons and equipment, as well as the condition of the roads—insofar as one can speak of roads at all—can be seen in the pictures. (BA)

Even the SPW, very well suited to cross-country travel, could hardly move forward. But they were needed to transport the wounded, and everybody helped out, including Russian civilians. (BA)

The men of the LAH are so pressed that every pause, no matter how short, was utilized. The motorcycle drivers nap on their cycles. (BA)

The picture at left symbolizes this defensive battle. An observation post beside a destroyed T 34 tank. (BA)

The winter makes the service conditions of the reduced LAH units even worse. (BA)

2nd Lieutenant
Herbert Walther
with the Corps-Tiger
Unit.

Transfer to the West to relax and take a new position in Belgium.

Above: Training of
junior leaders under
the supervision of
the Commander, SS
Major Hein von
Westernhagen, third
from left.

The Corps-Tiger Unit is set up
in the Mons area. The tanks bear
the crossed Dietrich with oak
leaves as their tactical emblem.

SERVICE IN NORMANDY

The Allied invasion on June 6, 1944 ended the short rest period. The "Bodyguard" was sent to Normandy on long-distance motorized marches, with heavy losses in men and material.

The Commander of the SS Armored Grenadier Regiment 1, Lieutenant Colonel Albert Frey, decorated with the Oak Leaf Cluster since December 20, 1943, and at that time Division Leader of the LAH, here receives a command that makes him first thoughtful, then skeptical, and finally forces him to a swift decision.

The first appearance of King Tiger tanks with the troops. Here they are well camouflaged in the park of Chateau de Canteloup. (BA)

SS Captain Michel Wittmann, SS Armored Unit 501, by far the most successful tank commander in World War II, stopped a breakthrough of the legendary African veterans, the "Desert Rats", near Villers-Bocage.

Above: Wittmann (left) with his men, at right his aiming specialist Balthasar Woll, likewise decorated with the Knight's Cross.

But even the Tigers were unable to cope with the enemy's material strength. Left: in the streets of Falaise. (BA)

A Tiger of the SS Armored Unit 501, destroyed by special bombs. (BA)

THE ARDENNES OFFENSIVE

The SS Armored Regiment 1 "LAH" had had a capable commander since November of 1943 in Jochen Peiper. The bold advance of his battle group with the results and the revenge of the later victors are forever linked with his name. On July 14, 1976, he was murdered in Traves, France. Thus he was the last man of the SS "Bodyguard" to fall.

An Allied air photo of a tank emplacement. (Robert Hunt Library)

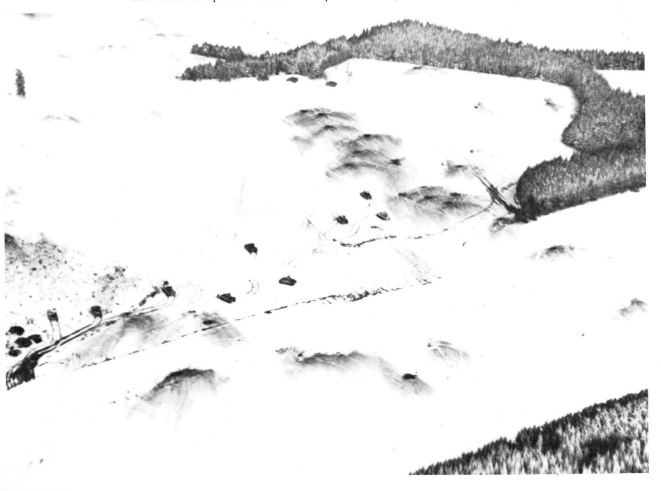

Grenadiers of the LAH in winter anoraks before a captured US armored scout car. The cigarettes must surely come from the "iron ration" of the captured tank. (BA)

Despite massive use of tanks and armored vehicles, the burden of fighting rests, as always, on the shoulders of the infantry, for only where it stands does the HKL stop or fall.

An infantryman examines a captured American halftrack. (BA)

After the defeat:

Past a forward-moving US column go young grenadiers taken prisoner, carrying a badly wounded comrade on their shoulders.

This fully destroyed tank symbolizes the failure of the "Watch on the Rhine" operation. (Robert Hunt Library)

THE END

In the spring of 1945, scarcely one-third of the 215 tanks with which the First SS Armored Division "LAH" had begun the Ardennes offensive were still more or less usable. The high casualties, especially of old "veterans", were made up to some extent by the transfer of superfluous Navy or Air Force men or those called up from munitions factories. Sepp Dietrich explained later at the Malmedy Trials: "They were more of a burden and had no concept of war as we knew it. We soon lost most of them."

Hitler, having gone back to die in the capital of his empire—the Russians were only about 100 kilometers from the gates of Berlin—ordered a relief attack of the 6th SS Armored Army under Sepp Dietrich against the Glan Bridgehead. The ultimate goal was the release of the troops surrounded in Budapest. This last attack of the Bodyguard was doomed to defeat from the start by the lack of heavy weapons, especially tanks, and particularly of fuel, against the vast superiority of the Russian forces. After initial successes, Sepp Dietrich ordered a retreat.

When this was reported to Hitler, he ordered Senior General Guderian, whom he had taken back into his good graces again, to have the Bodyguard immediately remove their sleeve stripes bearing his name. Sepp Dietrich did not bother to do so.

In English publications the nonsensical story appears over and over that the surviving, highly decorated leaders of the LAH had sent their decorations back to Hitler, appropriately in a chamberpot. This is complete nonsense. At that time it scarcely would have been possible anyway.

In an orderly retreat with their few remaining vehicles, the LAH moved westward. Small groups of them performed self-sacrificing delaying actions against the numerically very superior Russian troops who came after them. The fact that Vienna was not, as Hitler commanded, destroyed by fighting in the city is an accomplishment of SS Supreme General and Senior General of the Waffen-SS Sepp Dietrich. It remained his last task in the lost war to see that as many as possible of his soldiers did not fall into the hands of the Russians. In his last report to Field Marshal Kesselring he wrote: "The troops, decimated to less than a third of their strength, without any supplies, must surrender. Tomorrow we are going into captivity with heads held high!"

As the Americans commanded, all vehicles had to bear white flags on the motorized march. Just short of the demarcation line they were removed, and the battered remains of the once-proud "Bodyguard" made one last parade past their revered commander into captivity.

After many difficulties that had to be faced later, since the men of the Waffen-SS were declared "inhuman" at the Nürnberg Trials, the members of the Division saw each other again only now and then. These were meetings in which they were able to tell of the fates of many lost comrades. Thousands of Bodyguard men gave their "Sepp" the last escort when he was buried in Ludwigsburg on April 21, 1966.

Marked with white cloths, vehicles of the "Bodyguard" drive into captivity.

This picture taken early in 1945 shows the SS General Sepp Dietrich with his Adjutant, Captain Hermann Weiser, who died as the result of a war injury at the age of 51 and is buried near his commander in Ludwigsburg.

Wilhelm Möhnke, decorated with the Knight's Cross on July 11, 1944 as Commander of the SS Armored Grenadier Regiment 26 "HJ", led the LAH Division in late 1944 and early 1945. He was one of the first to join the LAH and, as SS Brigadier General, was the Commandant of the Chancellery in Berlin during April and May of 1945.

Hitler surely could not have known that the man at whom he is looking (4th from left, Wilhelm Möhnke as Commander of the 4th Company) would defend his bunker ten years later, in May of 1945. (BA)

As of February 1945, Otto Krumm, experienced troop leader of the regiment "Der Führer" and Commander of the 7th SS Mountain Division "Prince Eugene", took over what remained of the "LAH" Division and led it to the end. (J. W. Schneider Archives)

A SOLDIER'S LIFE

Alfred Miegel, a Berliner trained as a baker and pastrycook, joined the LAH in peacetime. In Metz during the summer of 1940 he received from Sepp Dietrich the storm emblem, after already having gained the Iron Cross II. At this time he was a Master Sergeant and Company Sergeant-Major. As a 1st Lieutenant, he led the First Section of the First SS Armored Fusilier Unit 1 LAH in the Battle of Kharkov.

Armored Fusilier "Marten" tanks of the Armored Fusilier Unit 1 LAH in Operation Citadel. (Worthmann)

In the spring of 1943 Alfred Miegel took command of the company and fell in the winter of 1943-44. He and his men were buried in a deep crater which was then filled in. The Russian winter covered his resting place forever.

SERVICE RECORD

Strengthened SS Regiment/Headquarters: Berlin Lichterfelde/ until September 1939 SS Brigade "LAH"/October 1939 to July 1940 Light SS Division (motorized)/1st SS Armored Division "LAH" from June 1941. Service of the 1st SS Armored Division

1939	September **Eastern Service**
	Advance of the strengthened SS Regiment "LAH" out of the Kreuzberg, Upper Silesia, area across the Warthe, Witawka, Mczzonow to near Warsaw. Battle on the Bzura and the Vistula Bend.

October to
1940	**Western Service**
May	Reorganization into SS Brigade "LAH" in Bad Ems and Rheine, Westphalia, advance into holland via Bentheim to the IJssel and Zwolle, taking of Rotterdam, Delft and The Hague, push through Belgium into France as far as Boulogne, turn to the south. Advance through Vichy to St. Etienne.

August to
1941
February	Reorganization into 1st SS Division (motorized) "LAH" in Metz, Lorraine.
March	Transfer to Bulgaria (Sofia).
April/ May	Advance through Yugoslavia to Greece. Taking of Kastoria, advance to the Peloponessus, taking of Patras.
	Eastern Service
June	Transfer for rest to the Brno and Prague areas. Reorganization into the 1st SS Armored Division LAH.
	1st Service:
July/ Sept.	Advance via Shitomir, Kiev, Uman, Dnepropetrovsk, Cherson to Perekop.
Sept./ Nov.	Turn to the east, advance to the coast of the Sea of Azov via Melitopol, Taganrog, to Rostov.

December to
1942
June	Defensive fighting on the Mius between Stepanovka and Taganrog.
July	Transfer to France.
	Western Service

August to
1943
January	Rest in Normandy
	Eastern Service
	2nd Service
February	Defensive fighting in the Kharkov area, evacuation of Kharkov.
March/ July	Retaking of Kharkov, advance to Byelogrod (Operation Citadel), Transfer to Italy.
	Southern Service
July/ Nov.	Securing the Upper Italian area.

November to
1944	Eastern Service (3rd Service)
March	Action west of the Dnieper, Shitomir-Berdichev, Winniza-Uman, Tscherkassy, Byela Zerkov. Retreat fighting (in the moving basin) "Hube Basin" via Proskurov to Tarnopol.
April	Transfer to the West.
	Western Service
April/ May	Rest in Belgium
June/ Sept.	Fighting on the invasion front, Caen-Falaise-Argentan area, tank battle around Mortain, breaking out of the basin of Falaise, retreat via Chambois, Rouen to Belgium/Beverloo, rest in the Siegburg area.

December to
1945
January Fighting near Losheim, Luneville-Stavelot, advance to Bastogne (Ardennes offensive), retreat via Malmedy, St. Vith, through the Eifel to the Bonn area.

Eastern Service (4th Service)

Feb./ **Fighting in Hungary over the Gran Bridgehead and near Stuhlweissenburg,**
April **retreat northwards of Plattensee via Neuhäusel, Coenburg, Wiener Neustadt to St. Pölten.**

May **Retreat to the Enns, surrender in the Steyr area, American imprisonment, portions turned over to the Russians.**

Text: Military Archives, Freiburg.

Ich hatt' einen Kameraden

In memory of my comrades of the Waffen-SS who died in battle, in imprisonment or of wounds.

ϟϟ-Kriegsberichter

Most of the pictures in this book were taken by men who wore this sleeve stripe. Often enough they fought, armed with MPi and Leica cameras, on the front lines and sought to document the rigors of the fighting through the lenses of their cameras. To them, and particularly to those who fell or were wounded, go my thanks.

They include, among others, Photojournalists Roth +, Augustin +, Büschel, Cantzler, Grönert, Jarolin, King, Weill and Zschäckel, as well as the Correspondent Artist Krause, whose drawings enrich this book.

120